Managing Client Expectations

A Guide for Organizing Professionals

Standolyn Robertson, CPO®

Copyright © 2020 Standolyn Robertson.

All rights reserved. No portion of this book may be reproduced mechanically, electronically, or by any other means, including photocopying, without the written permission of the publisher. It is illegal to copy this book, post it to a website, or distribute it by any other means without permission from the publisher.

> Things In Place®
>
> Los Angeles, California
>
> Email: Standolyn@thingsinplace.com
>
> Website: www.ThingsInPlace.com
>
>   www.Standolyn.com

Limits of Liability and Disclaimer of Warranty

The author and publisher shall not be liable for your misuse of this material. This book is strictly for informational and educational purposes.

Warning – Disclaimer

The purpose of this book is to educate, inspire and entertain. The author and publisher do not guarantee that anyone following these techniques, suggestions, tips, ideas, or strategies will become successful. The author and publisher shall have neither liability nor responsibility to anyone with respect to any loss or damage caused, or alleged to be caused, directly or indirectly by the information contained in this book. For situations outside of your expertise, refer the client to another professional with the relevant knowledge to handle the job. Always keep health and safety issues in mind for you and the client.

ISBN: 978-1796672305

Cover art copyright © 2020

Acknowledgments

Family is not an important thing. It's everything.

— Michael J. Fox —

My loving appreciation to the following individuals for believing in me:

Jamie Robertson, my husband, who consistently holds the point for me when I'm too close to see it. Your love and support are always evident in my life.

My sons, Seth and Erik, who are the loves of my life and keep me beaming with pride. Having a hand in raising you two can't be topped; thanks for your loving support.

This book is dedicated to my parents, who fostered my creativity and, in my childhood, provided me a loving environment where I had the freedom to play "real" house instead of "play" house to hone the skills that became the foundation of my business today.

Thanks to my clients and colleagues, who keep me on my toes.

To Geralin Thomas, Janine Adams, Margaret Lukens, Barry Izsak, and Val Sgro for convincing me that if I liked telling my story from the stage, I could also put pen to paper to tell it.

To Amber Vazquez, Michelle Menechyan, Leslie Limon, Denslow Brown, Donna Kozik, Amy Bowles, Jen Hadraba, Hazel Thornton, Julie Bestry, Hannah Sias, and Anne Holmberg for their roles as checkers, curators, and cheerleaders.

To all of my NAPO, ICD, and NASMM colleagues who sent me words of encouragement after attending one of my presentations. Thank you.

And finally, to the patient Shawndra Holmberg, the remarkable book coach for her knowledge, wisdom, and direction in the writing process.

She's the sole reason you are finally getting to read *Managing Client Expectations for Organizing Professionals*. She figured out how to get me to dust off a ten-year-old manuscript and finally get it out the door.

Contents

Acknowledgments v
Preface vii
Introduction ix
How to Use This Book xi

Stage 1 1
   What's Everybody Thinking? 3
   Keep it Open 5
   Our Profession 7
   Your Team 9
   Measures of Success 11
   Time Frame 15
   Priority 19
   Triggers and Red Flags 23
   Complexities 27
   Support Systems 29
   Session Scenario: Walk, Talk, Do, and Review 31
   Mental Focus and Physical Stamina 35
   Contracts, Agreements, Policies, and Procedures 39
   Appointment Setting 43
   Perfectionism 45

Stage 2 47
   Keep the Focus 49
   The Focus Has Changed 51
   Mutual Respect and Value Judgments 53
   Boundaries 57

    Making Suggestions 61

    Timekeeping... 63

    Remembering... 65

    Listen to Input 67

    Finish on a High Note 69

    Invoicing 73

Stage 3 75

    The Cost of Doing Business 77

    The Car Hostage 79

    Dressing the Part... 81

    Organizers' Expectations 85

    Follow-Up 87

    Self-Care 91

    Now What? 93

Traits Trusted Advisors Have in Common 95

Resources.. 97

About the Author 99

Preface

Have you replayed a client session after the appointment? Are you often grappling with what could have been done differently during the session to change the outcome? Maybe you're wondering what went wrong, how you could have avoided the awkwardness of talking your way out of a misunderstanding. Do you wonder why, despite your best intentions, you face the same dragon at every appointment?

This book is a step-by-step guide to managing your clients' expectations once and for all. This is the system I use in my business. This book explores the three critical stages of the client relationship.

Stage 1: The Beginning of the Relationship

Stage 2: The Middle: The Initial Client Contact

Stage 3: The End of the Appointment and the Beginning of a Lasting Relationship

I developed this system after the first time I felt frustrated following a client session. I dedicated much of my early career as a professional organizer to honing my skills in managing client relationships. I have often talked about the importance of managing client expectations and I have shared my system with colleagues from all over the world. Whether they have been in business for two weeks or twenty years, they all walked away with new insights on managing client expectations and how it would affect their day-to-day business.

If you are ready to see your client relationships thrive, read on to discover the skills, insights, and strategies that can empower you to take your business and client relations to a whole new level.

Introduction

A master can tell you what he expects of you. A teacher, though, awakens your own expectations.

— Patricia Neal —

Each time we begin working with a new client, we embark on what is for them a new road: a new perspective on an existing situation. The need to manage expectations—the client's and ours—exists from the moment we start down that road. Success in those relationships means managing the expectations of the organizer, the client, and the process. Set the expectations before the first appointment, and you will build the relationship on a solid foundation.

Early in my career as a professional organizer, a networking colleague referred a potential client to me. I immediately called, and we set up an appointment for the next day. (Back then clients had no trouble securing a next-day appointment with me.) She explained she was having a hard time with paper, and I figured, since I considered myself a paper expert, I could help her. I kept patting myself on the back for convincing her to use my services and getting off the phone in less than ten minutes. The next day, I got out of my car and approached the house with as much confidence as I could muster as a new organizer. After a few knocks, she greeted me, and I immediately asked for a tour of the house, because I heard the tour is one of the first things you want to do when you start a new project. After a quick view of the entry hall, we headed straight for the primary bedroom.

The first peek was the closet. The client started by stating, "I have a hard time fitting all of my things in this closet." We brainstormed solutions for using the space more effectively and continued to talk about this one closet for a solid hour. Thrilled with my suggestions, confident and proud of my work we moved on to the kitchen.

Here we found piles of paper. After all, that's why my client originally called me. We went through paper for the next two hours. As we finished up, I felt proud of the day's accomplishments.

Before I could finish the invoice, she wrote me a check for two hours of organizing services. Hiding my shock and disbelief, rather than argue the point, I took my check and made the long walk back to my car. I sat and wondered, "What happened? Where did I go wrong?" I was there for three hours but only got paid for two.

On the drive home, I replayed the session and realized it was me, not the client, who was at fault. She called for help with paper; I was the one who zigzagged through the house and lost my focus. I was the one who got stuck in the closet and thought it would be a fun project to tackle. In her mind, we spent an hour "talking" about the closet, not "organizing" it. We were just "talking," so I was not getting paid for that hour.

Underlying assumptions may announce themselves with a red flag, or they may be less obvious, but they must be anticipated. Either way, dealing with a situation where the client is unclear whether I'm on the clock or off is not about manipulating the client into paying me just to talk. Nor is it about making them think about a project "our way." It is, rather about having them realize that talking is a very important part of the process. It is about using my knowledge and expertise to foresee and sidestep roadblocks, revise unrealistic expectations, and debunk myths about working with a professional organizer.

Managing Client Expectations: A Guide for Organizing Professionals will give you tools to help avoid falling into a costly trap of misunderstanding, miscommunication, and other uncomfortable situations.

How to Use This Book

*The expectations of life depend upon diligence;
the mechanic that would perfect his work must
first sharpen his tools.*

— Confucius —

Managing Client Expectations will focus on techniques to manage client expectations through conversation.

Since I can't cover everything in this book, my goal is to inspire you to think about your conversations, help you personalize your style, and point you in a productive direction. I want to get the conversation *started*. You finish it in a manner that suits the missions for your practice. We will not debate the pros and cons of having contracts or engagement letters, how to write policies and procedures, or whether an assessment should be complimentary or fee-based. My purpose is to share my knowledge and get you thinking of your own process.

At the end of each topic there will be one or more of the following:

 Pro Tips — additional tips and highlights.

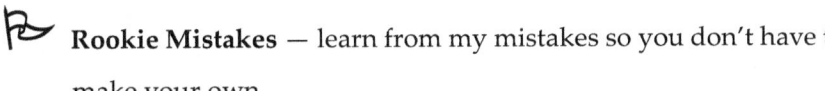 **Rookie Mistakes** — learn from my mistakes so you don't have to make your own.

Power Questions — powerful questions to use with your clients.

Business Strategies — questions to ask and thoughts to think about your business to develop strategies, policies, procedures to build your business.

Stage 1

The Beginning

Life is largely a matter of expectation.

— Horace —

Stage 1 establishes the beginning of the relationship with your potential client by unveiling what everyone is bringing to the table. Once you get the client to disclose their vision, timeline, support systems, and measures of success, you are better equipped to define your working relationship. Getting a potential client to share their fears, concerns, and goals conversationally will set you apart from colleagues who don't have client-centered practices. We will explore ways to identify the information you need to determine if this relationship is a good fit for your business.

Stage 1: The Beginning

What's Everybody Thinking?

Always aim at complete harmony of thought and word and deed. Always aim at purifying your thoughts and everything will be well.

— Mahatma Gandhi —

Before you start a project with a client, the first step is to understand your client's expectations. For me this happens on the phone; for others, it may be an in-person meeting. Do most of the fact-finding and relationship developing in Stage 1 before the first hands-on session. This is where the magic starts.

Think about the standard questions you routinely ask. Are they helping you understand the client's needs? Use a checklist to make sure you cover key issues during the initial conversation. It's essential to hit key points without sounding as if you are reading a checklist, so weave in your questions while keeping the discussion conversational.

Keeping the interview casual involves active listening and asking open-ended questions, which I will talk more about in the next chapter. You don't want to sound like a two-year-old. (Why, why, why?) Ask a few questions then listen. Ask a few more questions and then listen more. A lot of what you want to know will be answered without you asking. You will check those off the list and move on.

Having a conversational interview is a skill you can hone with every call. It allows you to assess the situation and build a relationship simultaneously. It will become second nature with practice. Listen for the client's buzzwords and weave them into your summaries of what they are conveying. When you use a client's language, the client knows you heard them.

Managing Client Expectations

Whether in person or on the phone, the key is to have the conversational interview before you start working together. You are laying the foundation for the whole relationship. You can't manage expectations if you don't know what a client is thinking.

What questions do you need to add to your assessment?

📌 Pro Tips

- Keep it conversational.
- Remember to listen actively.

🚩 Rookie Mistakes:

- Not asking about parking.
- Not prepared for a "no show" home.
- Not asking about guns, porn, exotic pets, and anything else that might be a deal breaker for you or give you pause.

True Story #1: I did not ask about parking. I ended up in a parking garage paying four times more than I expected. Now I always ask.

True Story #2: I don't mind snakes, but I'm uncomfortable around rats. I worked with a teen who had two large pet rats walking around the room while we worked.

🛠 Business Strategies

- ❑ Visualize how your phone session will flow.
- ❑ Develop a list of questions to ask potential clients.
- ❑ What questions do you need to add to your assessment?
- ❑ Use a client's language; the client will know you heard them.

Keep it Open

My advice is to be very careful about doing any project that hasn't been thoroughly scoped out in advance, even if you're starving for work. By 'thoroughly' I mean that you, the client, your mom and your dog all know in fairly granular detail what's expected and when.

— Keith Robinson —

Open-ended questions let the conversation focus on what's important to the client.

Businessman Robert Half reminds us "asking the right questions takes as much skill as giving the right answers." Your goal here is to stay away from yes or no questions. Offering open-ended prompts will not only help you get the answers you need to assess the situation but will get the client talking.

Give the potential client ample opportunity to speak, and give yourself sufficient time to listen and digest what you're hearing. An open-ended question allows you to get more information out of a client's response.

Open with the following:

Tell me about...

How can I help you?

What are your goals for the project?

If you do use yes or no questions, follow up using these words to move things along:

- What
- Why
- How

📌 Pro Tip

Avoid putting potential clients into defense mode. There's an art to *what*, *why*, and *how* questions. Ask open ended questions to get more out of the conversation.

> Open-ended: **What** would you want to change in this space?
> Closed-ended: Do you like this space?

> Open-ended: **Why** is it important to get organized now?
> Closed-ended: Have you always been disorganized?

> Open-ended: **How** would this fit into your goal?
> Closed-ended: Do you want this?

💥 Power Questions

- Tell me about...
- How can I help you?
- What are your goals for the project?
- If you do use yes or no questions, follow up using these words to move things along: What? Why? How?

🛠 Business Strategy

- ☐ Review your assessment and, where appropriate, make the questions open-ended.

Our Profession

Simplicity is the ultimate sophistication.

— Leonardo DaVinci —

Clients come to the table with preconceived assumptions and expectations, even before they call us.

Find out what a prospective client knows about our profession. Give clients a chance to reflect on and voice their notions of what you can do for them. As you talk through all aspects of the project, weave in questions like these:

"What do you know about the organizing profession?"

> Listen for cues suggesting the client sees you as a "miracle worker" or "savior." Spell out, realistically and accurately, what you expect to deliver.

"Is this your first time working with a professional organizer?"

> No need to dwell on past experiences, but use the answer as an opportunity to explain what they can expect from *this* relationship.

"What are some of your fears of working with an organizer?"

> If the client is concerned you will make them throw out all of their belongings, you can reassure the client you will help them let go of the things they no longer want. Address the client's concerns about getting rid of things. You can often point out that you can help them use space more efficiently and find homes for the things they value most.
>
> If your client ends up needing a dumpster, by the time you need to order it, the trust between you and your client will be at a higher

level than it was before the first few appointments. The dumpster may even represent something positive rather than negative.

Power Questions

- What do you know about the organizing profession?
- Is this your first time working with a professional organizer?
- What are some of your fears of working with an organizer?

Stage 1: The Beginning

Your Team

The way a team plays as a whole determines its success. You may have the greatest bunch of individual stars in the world, but if they don't play together, the club won't be worth a dime.

— Babe Ruth —

You want to give the client a clear understanding of the makeup of your team, what your resources are, and what to expect. The client needs to be comfortable with the entire team, from the lead organizer to the assistant sorter and dumpster haulers.

In most of my routine work, I'm alone or with a small group of organizers and assistants. Make sure new additions to the team are just as suitable to work with the client as you are. More than just liking our websites, clients pick us for many more reasons than we realize — some that are not mentioned earlier; therefore, you may not be familiar with some of the quirks of the selection process.

I had a client who did not want to work with anyone in her town, nor anyone she'd either worked with, or chosen not to work with, before hiring my company. It was vital for her to know the names of every employee and subcontractor I brought to the project. I learned this lesson the hard way when I forgot to check with her before I brought in another organizer to assist on the project. It ended up working out, but not without the two of us having a long talk.

I put my client in an awkward position. She had to confront me and remind me of her original request. I did not stick to my initial commitment to discuss whom I brought into her home. Luckily, we resolved it, but it could have cost me the job.

Your "team" may also include carpenters, electricians, plumbers, and other contractors. I offer a resource list to my clients, but the client makes the final choice. The client deals with the contractor independently from the work I do with them. Remind your client that unlike in makeover shows, no electrician is waiting out in the truck to install an outlet near a computer station or a carpenter who's always available to put in shelves the same day we decide to add them. In reality, a carpenter or electrician may not show up for weeks.

Pro Tip

Make every project a team effort. Whether it's just the client and yourself, or ten others, always collaborate for success.

Business Strategies

- ❏ Dig deeper to find the source of the client's concern and then address it.
- ❏ Create an extensive resource list with a variety of choices.

Measures of Success

*The only true measure of success
is the amount of joy we are feeling.*

— Esther Hicks —

At some point during the initial consultation, the prospective client will express a goal to get organized by announcing, "I want/need to get organized." Find out what it means to get organized. Start by asking questions. Do your homework and figure out what is essential to the client, then establish realistic goals based on the client's expectations for getting organized. Plan to meet your client's expectations for success, not yours.

I had a client who wanted her grandkids to sit on the couch for Mother's Day. My natural inclination was to sort everything in the room into categories before tackling pieces of furniture. The client just wanted her daughter, son-in-law, and grandkids to sit on the couch; she did not care how the rest of the room looked. We started with the sofa, then moved on to the chairs. We eventually did the coffee and end tables, then the floor. A few months later I realized there was a fireplace in the room. Would I tackle the room the same way today? Most likely not, but what I know for sure is, I would honor her goal to have clear seating, then continue to work in the space with that goal in mind. The cool benefit of this is now she has an easily identifiable target with which to measure her success. Asking herself if there is seating for Sunday visits and a clear path to the seating is much easier to measure than if the room is "organized."

Another example: I worked with a new client for three hours, and all we did was the counter. By my standards the progress was slow. The client was thrilled with the results and repeatedly said "Oh, my goodness. The counter is done. I can't believe it. The counter is done."

Managing Client Expectations

Knowing why she wants clear counters is helpful, too. Finding out it's a space to bake more with grandkids, pay bills, do jigsaw puzzles, and display flowers from the garden becomes the success. Follow up is not about "is your kitchen still organized," it is about being able to bake and decorate cookies during the holidays and have a clear spot to get bills out on time and enjoy jigsaw puzzles with a partner every Sunday.

Professional organizers often have to slow down and resist the impulse to start planning immediately. We know how we want a room to function, but it may not invariably be what the client needs. You want to give the client what's ideal for them so the client feels successful in the space. Work smart and find out what's important to your client. Set your expectations aside. At the end of the day, you want to be able to check the box that reflects their goals. Measuring your success not only consists of focusing on the smaller project at hand that's important to the client, but also breaking down their broader goals to abide by the project scope. Sometimes the client's ambitious goals are more than what you can accomplish in one session. Therefore, you may have to take a 12-hour project and chunk it down to four 3-hour sessions. Chunk down the successes accordingly. Remember, the appointment is not about you; it's the client's time.

Ask: "What does the finished space look like to you?"

The answer will help you envision what the client expects. Maybe it matches visible results they saw in a magazine. Before you start, address the realities of redecorating, carpentry, and furniture. Align the client's expectations with the scope of the project and their budget.

If the client describes a project with new furniture and new paint, it begins to sound more like they want a decorator than a professional organizer. You may be qualified to do both, but you need to be clear about why you are being called in on this project. Here you have an opportunity to explain the organizing process, creating workflow systems and establishing how things will work long after you finish. Talk about investing in furniture to store only the items they choose to keep. For example, the wall of file cabinets the client initially envisioned before working with you is down to one drawer of resource files. This conversation alone can save the client time and money.

Here's your opportunity to communicate the benefits of getting organized before the client retains the services of an interior designer. Never assume what "organized" looks like for the client.

Ask: "How do you want to feel in the finished space?"

Their response will help you guide them in creating a mood for the space. Listen for words like: productive, calm, relaxed, fun, creative. If you're working in an art studio, organized tools will make it easier to get started and spark more creative activity. Or consider an organized rec room where the games are in place, and the focus is on fun rather than the stress of clutter and missing game pieces.

Asking questions will help you find out what the project will look and feel like on the client's terms. Continue to develop the skills that keep the focus on the client's goals, not yours. Use those goals to establish measures of success for the session as well as the project.

📌 Pro Tip

Figure out what is important to the client in order to establish realistic goals based on the client's expectations.

You guide, they decide.

Managing Client Expectations

🚩 Rookie Mistake

Early in my professional organizing career, I saw a hornets' nest of a filing system on a new client's kitchen counter. Without even asking her, I assumed that "fixing it" was high on her priority list. It took some discussion to discover she was proud of her countertop system, which she felt met her needs just fine. By focusing on the wrong thing, I missed an early opportunity to discuss what was really bugging her.

Over time, she tweaked her countertop system based on the new skills she developed by working with me, and I made patience a crucial part of my professional bag of tricks.

💥 Power Questions

- *What does the finished space look like to you?*
- *How do you want to feel in the finished space?*

🛠 Business Strategies

You have the opportunity to clarify the distinctions between decorators and organizers and have a working relationship with an interior designer.

Talking Points: Why working with a professional organizer before an interior designer is hired makes it easier:

- ❏ to visualize and get "the look" when the distractions are gone
- ❏ to get back up and running after a paint and furniture update
- ❏ for contractors to work in spaces with clear paths and space to keep supplies close at hand

Time Frame

*Judge your success by what you had
to give up in order to get it.*

— Dalai Lama —

Does the client seem concerned about impending deadlines? When a potential client is motivated, they are inclined to want the project done right away.

Their Time

Getting organized becomes an emergency situation in many people's lives. By establishing the reasons the client wants to get organized now, you can better serve them. Is the client calling you because their daughter is getting married in a month and they want the house presentable for guests? Alternatively, is this a case where a landlord has given the client a deadline to clean up or get out? Are they catching heat from their boss? If you're not available for three weeks and the client is on a strict deadline, you need to make it clear in the preliminary phone consultation.

Lifestyle networks and the media have done an excellent job of bringing awareness to our industry, but they have also set up unrealistic expectations around project timing. During the phone assessment, ask potential clients if they have seen organizing shows on television. If so, explain there's more to the process than can be seen in a 30-minute TV show. Many clients can get discouraged because they are overwhelmed and everything seems to take a long time, but this gives you the chance to discuss a realistic time frame for their project.

Managing Client Expectations

Your Time

Another concern is allowing a client to convince you to work a schedule not aligned with your business hours to meet their time-frame. You can't blame the client for your time conflicts. Since this relationship might not be a winning match, find someone to whom you can refer them that will be a better fit for the client's time-frame requirements.

Don't get upset if a new client called late in the evening if you are picking up your phone at 9:30 p.m. Consider they may have assumed the office was closed and simply thought they could leave a message. Do you charge extra for working outside your regular work hours? Set your guidelines and boundaries for working weekends, holidays, overtime, and rush jobs.

Your business policies and procedures must be in line with the client's expectations. To avoid conflict, set realistic timeline expectations and concrete schedules.

📌 Pro Tip

Set business hours and follow them.

🛠 Business Strategies

- ❑ Establish your guidelines and boundaries for working:
    - o weekends
    - o holidays
    - o overtime
    - o rush jobs
    - o make-up work (redo a job)
- ❑ Do you charge extra for working outside your regular work hours?

Priority

*Organization is what you do before you do it so
when you do it, it's not all messed up.*

— Winnie the Pooh —

Look at the project's **scope**, **schedule**, and **cost** to help you determine the client's priorities.

These aspects of the project can be fixed, semi-fixed, or flexible, but each aspect can only be one of those. For example, if the client has a strict schedule for completing the project, then the **schedule** is fixed. That means the **scope** and **cost** must be semi-fixed or flexible; not everything can be fixed.

Here is an example of how that would work.

A potential client calls on May 5th saying she just found out her mother-in-law will arrive on an afternoon flight from Florida on May 9th to live with them. She says, "I need you to take my office, which I've had in the spare bedroom for fifteen years, and move it to the dining room. I would also like the dining room to be available in the evening, but it will have to function as a full-service office during the day."

Scope: To set up a spare bedroom and a dining room which serves as an office during the day and a space for dining in the evening

Schedule: 4 days

You now have a responsibility to point out the firm deadline is in conflict with their expectation of having a fixed scope. For example, that may mean you saying, "I'll have your office in the dining room, and your mother-in-law will have a place to lay her head, but you may not have the office you described in four days."

Cost: Per their budget

You could determine the cost of the project ahead of time. She could give you a firm budget, or you could leave it open and see how many hours the project will take. Bringing in a team of organizers on weekends or hiring movers at the end of the month can both increase the cost of the project.

By strategizing, you have the opportunity to establish which is the highest priority to the client.

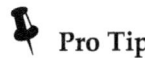 **Pro Tip**

Use a Priority Grid

	Scope	Schedule	Cost
Fixed		X	
Semi-Fixed	X		
Flexible			X

The grid is not something you would share with a client. It's used here to illustrate a point. It is a tool to help you manage expectations from the outset.

You might say to your client, "In order for me to have the project done by May 9th without anyone being disappointed, we have to work together and see where we can be flexible." Perhaps she may become more flexible on the expenses, meaning you can bring in five more people to make the whole project happen according to her time restraints. Maybe the schedule isn't as fixed as it seemed at first.

Find out where you have some wiggle room so you can set up a situation where everyone feels the project was successful in the end. Align the client's expectations with the **scope** of the project, the time frame (**schedule**), and the client's budget (**cost**).

Triggers and Red Flags

...The people you're communicating with may not understand what you mean. You can't be sure you'll meet each other's expectations if your very words confuse, annoy, or intimidate.

— Naomi Karten —

Managing client expectations requires an awareness of a client's emotions, especially during the first appointment. Never assume the client's reason for calling you is always the real issue. If you can figure out a client's triggers and sensitive topics, you'll be better prepared to help them refocus on their current goals if and when those triggers come up. As you develop your interpersonal skills, you'll be able to tell when there's a shift in a client's thinking, and you can be more supportive during those sensitive times.

Triggers

In sales, you often hear "find the pain." I don't like the sound of that as theintention seems negative. I think of it as "finding the gap" between the situation they're in now and where they will be upon project completion.

As an example, your client envisioned having her bedroom closet organized before having her sister move into her small rental. You walk into the bedroom and see piles of clothes on the floor with no space in the closet or drawers. Rather than focusing on the task at hand, the client focuses on her divorce, her ADHD, losing her walk-in-closet when she was forced to move out of her much larger house. The piles of clothes are the trigger, which affect the client's emotions because it represents the gap between who they are now, and who they want to be when they reach their organizing goals. There's an opportunity here to defuse the situation. Don't define the client by the situation they are in now. Help them focus on where they are going and not where they have been.

Those piles of clothes followed by tears may represent the unfinished projects and lack of space all over the rental. Here is your opportunity to offer positive reassurance and help them maintain focus. Organizing can be a daunting—even overwhelming—experience. Some clients resent needing outside help to organize their belongings. Be clear about your own expectations of how you can manage the client's emotions during this challenging transition.

No matter what your level of expertise, remember you are not a therapist. However, you can continue to hone your interpersonal skills. This personal development will better prepare you to handle the client's emotions and boundary issues.

Red Flags

If you see or hear red flags, you may need to refer to a specialist for this project. Warning signs may include a client saying "I just can't let anything go," "I'm not sleeping at night," or "I can't seem to focus." Another red flag could be the client mentioning that someone else wants them to get organized. If you listen for specific cues in the conversation that raise red flags, you'll be able to recognize when you need to find help. Many organizers have their specialties catering to different needs of clients. If a client's situation is not within your area of expertise and you are not trained to work on these complex projects, you can do more damage than good by ignoring the warning signs. Do not get in over your head.

Stage 1: The Beginning

📌 Pro Tip

Be careful what you say. Using phrases like those below could trigger an emotional response or bring about false or unrealistic expectations:

- It's clear to me you're a level....

    Using technical jargon to label a client is inappropriate.

- What were you thinking?

    This question has a negative tone.

    Try asking "How does this align with your goals?"

- Clients always....

    Don't generalize. Every situation is unique.

- It's obvious you need to....

    Implying something is obvious makes it seem like the client missed it or they should've known.

- My goal for you is....

    Your goal is to help them realize their goals.

- We will get a dumpster and throw this junk out.

    This has a negative connotation to refer to the client's things as junk. Wait to introduce a dumpster until you've established enough trust in the working relationship.

Can you think of others?

🚩 Rookie Mistake

Trying to diagnose a client without the proper credentials.

Managing Client Expectations

✖ Business Strategies

What warning signs raise red flags in your business? What health and safety issues or physical/mental challenges do you already look for? Are you clear when it's best to refer clients to another professional?

- ❏ Mold
- ❏ Water damage
- ❏ Animal waste
- ❏ Piles above waist-height
- ❏ Blocked exits
- ❏ Fire hazards
- ❏ Rodent infestation
- ❏ No outside light in the home
- ❏ Mental health issues
- ❏ Depression
- ❏ Erratic behavior

Complexities

*Life is really simple,
but we insist on making it complicated.*

— Confucius —

Every project is different, but with practice, you will start to hear the clues you need to determine the intricacy of a project during your initial consultation. You'll recognize keywords; you'll understand what specific phrases mean and how you can use them to determine the project complexities and avoid getting in over your head.

Even with a lot of practice you may start a job and discover the situation is different than you anticipated. Make a note of the questions you should have asked but didn't, then add these to your intake. No one wants to show up for work and realize they should have worn protective clothing to enter the home. Or think they're going to clear up some computer clutter and realize the client was looking to put in an entirely new Customer Relationship Management (CRM) system for their business.

Continue to expand your resource list. Look to your colleagues and networking groups for specialties different from yours. Don't forget, with computer technology and the ease of screen sharing, your options are not limited to your geographical location.

Specialists to add to your Resource List:

Bio Hazard	Moving & Downsizing
Brain Injury	Pest Management
Chronic Disorganization	Photo Organizing
Financial	Technology, General
Hoarding	Technology, Sensitive Content
Mental Health	Waste Management

Managing Client Expectations

🏴 Rookie Mistake

Being unprepared to offer solutions or resources for complex issues. Don't be caught off guard. Be prepared to point the client to someone who can address their needs.

💥 Power Question

- *Do you have someone to help you with that?*

🛠 Business Strategies

- ❏ What situations should you anticipate?
- ❏ What's the best way to approach the challenge?
- ❏ Identify resources to add to your Resource List.
- ❏ Update or add intake questions after any session turns out to be more complex than expected.

Support Systems

Spread love everywhere you go. Let no one ever come to you without leaving happier.

— Mother Teresa —

Early in the first conversation, in a neutral tone, ask "What is your support system?"

Some people will say, "My wife is supportive of this project." That's good information because now you know their partner will not sabotage the client's efforts.

Maybe you'll hear "I have a supportive mother, and she comes over three times a week and helps me with the kids." Now you know the client can focus on the project without interruptions.

The client may also say, "I'm seeing a therapist for my depression." That's good information, but the secret is that you didn't ask, "Hey are you seeing a therapist?" You asked, "What's your support system?"

Whatever answer they give you is right for now. The client has given you as much as they can share, and that's fine. The client will share more as the relationship develops.

On the other hand, if someone has concerns about acquiring and refers to themselves as a shopaholic or a packrat, I feel comfortable asking if they're working with a therapist now. In certain situations, I let them know I prefer a collaborative relationship with a healthcare provider before we embark on a new relationship together.

An organizer once told me she worked with a client who had no support. If you're ever in a situation where a client feels like they have no support, brainstorm ways to build their team while working with them. These support systems vary and can include therapists, accountants, virtual assistants, or even a well-intentioned family member or friend.

Once you understand a client's support system, you can use the information to set boundaries, manage expectations, and guide the client to the appropriate person for support. I like to think of everyone the client uses as support as a team member. Once I understand the team, I can help my client use them effectively. For example, if my client is extra chatty during an appointment, I can point out that talking about family dynamic frustrations with a therapist, or lack of energy with their physician, and focusing on the hands-on aspects of organizing a project with me would be a better use of our time together.

Pro Tip

Relationship-building takes time. Make sure you ask all the questions you need to feel comfortable taking on the job.

Power Question

- *What's your support system?*

Business Strategy

- ❏ What can you add to your assessment to get useful information about the work you will do with a client?

Session Scenario:
Walk, Talk, Do, and Review

There are no secrets to success. It is the result of preparation, hard work, and learning from failure.

— Colin Powell —

Before the first in-person session with a client, describe the upcoming meeting, from start to finish: **walk, talk, do,** and **review**. I call this process *previewing expectations*. Although I did not originate this concept—it's used in classrooms by teachers to help students know what to expect—I love it because it ensures there are no unexpected moves for the client and helps me better manage the session. You will often need to go into more depth previewing the first session because it's the first time they have worked with a professional organizer. If anything significant changes about the routine on later appointments, I preview expectations again.

Scenario: First In-Person Session

Begin the session by taking a walking tour of the space. This is the **walk**. This lets you make visual observations, scout new storage possibilities, and formulate a strategy. On later visits, you can often omit this step and jump right into talking about the strategy for the session.

After the tour, have a five to twenty-minute strategy session to discuss and agree on a plan of attack. This is the **talk**. During this strategy session, you're not sorting belongings or shuffling papers. You're just talking, but this is still organizing. This helps clients understand that if you are discussing the project, you are working, even if you are not handling their things.

The **do** portion of the session is where you will concentrate the bulk of the appointment time. Whether working desk-side, sorting, purging, determining what will go or stay, this segment is where the client experiences hands-on work and where most of the tangible changes take place. Here's where you're turning the strategy into action and the goals come alive.

Don't underestimate the significance of the pre-work you have done to strengthen the **do** portion of appointment with clients.

You will need to develop transition techniques, including a standard routine for ending sessions. Let your clients know you will do a walk-through "show and tell" to list accomplishments, **review** how the implemented system works, and discuss strategies for sustaining it. Solicit the client's help in listing the session's accomplishments so they can tell you all the things you've done together. Write these on the invoice. Then set the next appointment and collect payment.

The **review** is a routine you both can look forward to and come to expect at the end of the session. The benefit to clients is gaining a sense of closure. The bonus is a definite end to the session. You get out the door on time instead of sitting around chatting after a finished session.

Billing for All 4 Steps

Of all of the four steps, clients more clearly visualize the **do** time. Often, you have to explain to them it's not going to be 3 hours of hands-on work and there will be other aspects to the session. The more you can educate your client about what to expect, the more they feel a part of the process.

It is essential clients understand strategizing is a critical component of organizing. Once I arrived at a client's home and she immediately recognized and apologized that she had forgotten to clear a spot for "the talk," a step she remembered from our phone conversation where I previewed the session steps. She knew from our phone conversation I would arrive, take a tour, and then sit to discuss the plan for the session. Besides the physical act of organizing, talking and consulting are essential for success. Here's where you share your expertise with the client.

Being in a helping profession doesn't mean ignoring any time you spend with the client. The time billed needs to cover the **walk**, **talk**, and the **review** as well as the **do**. Clients understand the physical act of organizing is a billable part of the session. They also need to understand strategizing on the project deserves equal billing during the session, too.

Setting Expectations

Before you actually start that first in-person session, give the client a run through during the initial phone call, so you both begin the in-person session with the end in mind. The scenario run-through of **walk**, **talk**, **do**, **review** before you even arrive helps the client know what to expect and provides a clear structure for the process.

Honor the routine and, remember, success here is no accident.

Managing Client Expectations

📌 Pro Tip

Either make or ask for suggestions for the best way to check in regarding the pace of the project.

⚡ Power Question

- *What do you suggest is the best way to check in regarding the pace of the project?*

⚒ Business Strategies

- ❏ Build your Session Scenario to share in the interview call.
- ❏ If you've gone paperless, do you have an electronic invoicing system that helps you manage client expectations?

Stage 1: The Beginning

Mental Focus and Physical Stamina

*If you cannot find it in yourself,
where will you go for it?*

— Chinese proverb —

Prepare clients for sessions. Reinforce you will be there for them and that you're the project manager. Let the client know you will do everything you can to keep the project on track and to follow through on goals. Review your expectations of your clients to ensure maximum use of your time with them by asking that they:

- Limit phone calls and text messaging unless it's an emergency.

- Make arrangements for childcare while you work together

- Ensure that pets are excluded or controlled during the session

Clients start the process knowing they have a partner rooting for their success. Here's where body doubling comes into play. There will be times when you become the energy-pack on the project. Here you stand in as a source of energy for the client when they lack the mental or physical stamina to move forward. Think of the Energizer Bunny mascot here—he just keeps going and going. A client can tap into your motivation and use it to get over the most challenging moments in the project. We can hold the point for clients when things seem hopeless and unattainable. Reminding clients about the impermanence of their current situation will help them move forward with more optimism.

Add value for your client by encouraging them to increase their focus and stamina by eating healthy, staying hydrated, and getting a good night's sleep. This reinforces that we will work hard, and it also helps to model how to prepare for a project when clients are working on their own.

Have you ever been working with a client and suddenly it seems as if they go blank? Maybe it's a migraine triggered by an empty stomach and exhaustion. Maybe their blood sugar dropped because they were trying to make it on the last bit of energy from last night's dinner. No matter how it was triggered, once you've lost the client, they're gone. Now it's awkward since you are on the clock and they are still paying for the session.

Colleagues sometimes ask, "You're telling your clients what to eat?" I don't tell clients to go out and get particular foods, but I urge them to eat what they consider a healthy meal. It's my way of clarifying that the session is mentally and physically taxing. Help clients recognize that they can make better decisions when they are clear-headed. Though I'm not a nutritionist, I doubt anyone could argue that eating a healthy meal and drinking water for hydration before a mentally and physically challenging workout would be harmful.

The same lessons pertain to you. You're part of the team, too, so you need to show up, prepared and well rested. It's essential that clients know that you will be fully present for them during the session. Get a good night's sleep and eat a good breakfast. Bring water, a snack and arrive at the appointment early so you have a few minutes outside to focus your thoughts on the client and the project goals.

📌 Pro Tip

Review your expectations for limiting distractions with clients to ensure they get the most out of the session.

- Phone calls and text messaging are limited.
- Child care is scheduled while you work together.
- Pets are excluded or controlled during the session.

🚩 Rookie Mistakes

- Showing up without water.
- Not having your own snacks.

True Story: I was working on an all-day job with a long-time client who always offered me food. I always followed my company policy and said no. One day, I was really hungry and I'd forgotten to bring my usual snack. I saw a box of chocolates. I was eyeing them and almost convinced myself it would be okay to have one. The client, who had just returned home from a mystical spiritual journey in another country, walked by the area I was working in and said, "don't eat those, the chocolates are laced with hallucinogenic mushrooms." To this day, I'm so thankful I stuck to my company policy of not eating food from a client's home.

Contracts, Agreements, Policies, and Procedures

Good order is the foundation of all things.

— Edmund Burke —

During the initial phone call, you should also spell out the guidelines for working with your company. Your new client should not be surprised to get a contract or letter of engagement in the mail from your company before the session. It's helpful to tell clients to expect something in their mailbox from you in the next few days. You might say, "In two days you'll get a client agreement in your inbox, and it will spell out everything we discussed during this call."

A new client should not find out about your cancellation policy by opening an email containing an invoice for a missed appointment without having a clear understanding of your company's policies and procedures before the first visit. In the unlikely event a client cancels an appointment, they should not be surprised to receive an invoice from your company for cancellation fees. I don't often get a cancellation so I rarely have to enforce the policy, but I take advantage of any opportunity to show that I take my business and time seriously.

If the client is surprised by anything in the process, then you have dropped the ball. Success starts with getting your expectations on the table before the first appointment. This can be done through a written or verbal contract, engagement letter, or agreement. Since projects are collaborative, both the organizer and the client need to agree on a process. In Stage 2, I will talk about when expectations change and how to address them.

Although we will not spend a lot of time discussing policies and procedures, it's important to differentiate the two. The difference between a policy and procedure is that the policy is strategic while the procedure is operational.

For example, your business may have a volunteer *policy* where you dedicate a certain number of complimentary hours to clients. Your *procedure* would outline the qualifications for potential clients such as having non-profit status, filling out a need-based application, and your scheduled days set aside for volunteer projects.

Another example is your business's snow day *policy*. This is a strategic decision you make in your company for safety reasons based on your location. The *procedure* includes the steps you take — for instance, if your town has a snow day, you will not drive and will call two hours before the appointment to let the client know.

Think of the policy as the rule and the procedures as steps you take to follow the rule.

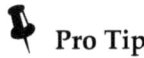 **Pro Tip**

Discuss the guidelines for working with your company during the initial phone call.

Business Strategies

- ☐ Do you have a snow day, pandemic or volunteer policy?
- ☐ Brainstorm company policies and procedures that will help you manage client expectations.
- ☐ Add any missing policies and procedures.
- ☐ Schedule an annual review of your policies and procedures.

Appointment Setting

With the new day,
comes new strength and new thoughts.

— Eleanor Roosevelt —

Appointment setting consists of getting the date and time in the calendar, confirming it with the client, and reinforcing the reminder policy.

Time management often comes up during the initial call, so you usually know what calendar system the client is using by the time you are ready to set an appointment. In a very conversational manner, you say, "I'll wait while you get the calendar." After settling on a date, say, "I reserved Wednesday, February 10th from 9:30 a.m. to 1:30 p.m." Then listen for their confirmation.

Some organizers will call the client a few days ahead of time to remind them of the appointment. I don't do that because I believe it's essential for the client to learn how to manage their time from the beginning of our relationship. This also frees me from the responsibility of making phone calls in the evening to remind clients of the appointment.

There are exceptions. For example, I have a monthly maintenance client who picks a new project every month. I send her a quick "What are the goals for tomorrow?" email the night before the appointment.

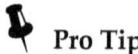

📌 Pro Tip

If your company's policy is to contact the client before the appointment, let them know to expect an email reminder or call one to two days before the scheduled meeting.

⚡ Power Question

- *I'll wait while you get your calendar.*

🛠 Business Strategies

- ❏ What's your cancellation policy? Is it in the contract?
- ❏ What will you do if you show up and they aren't there, they forgot, or they want to cancel?

Perfectionism

Have no fear of perfection — you'll never reach it.

— Salvador Dali —

I don't have all of my spices in alphabetical order, and I rarely get into this level of detail with clients. My job is to move the project forward without getting lost in the smallest details.

A client who is a perfectionist may hyper-focus on one aspect of the project and then be disappointed with the progress of the project. Many times, you learn of a client's perfectionism through hearing about their many false starts, unrealistic time expectations, over-use of "should," and their focus on things that add little value to the bigger project.

From the outside, it may be hard to understand how a perfectionist can be disorganized. We often think of perfectionists as having everything just right. Here's why that doesn't play out as well in real life: Once the perfectionist client starts hyper-focusing on one aspect of any task, they fall behind on everything else, or they don't even bother to start the project because it will never be done to meet their expectations.

By establishing, from the beginning, that you're not a perfectionist and *everything* won't be perfect, the client has the opportunity to see the progress on a higher level. Reinforce "good enough" results rather than "perfect outcomes" for the project. Remember, they hired you to be the project manager, so managing how the perfectionist uses their time is paramount for job success.

Managing Client Expectations

📌 **Pro Tip**

Our goal is to get donations out of the house. Help your clients who struggle with finding the perfect charity by suggesting they "trust that the right people will find the items."

Be careful of armchair diagnosis and don't label a client that has not been seen by a professional. A client may arbitrarily throw around words about themselves such as OCD, anal-retentive, or a perfectionist. Your job is to stay focused on the goals, not the labels.

💥 **Power Question**

- *I know this is not ideal. What can we do for now?*

🛠 **Business Strategy**

- ❏ Develop your Power Questions and Power Statements to keep the project moving forward.

Stage 2

The Middle

You're in. Now you will switch from proving you're the expert to proving you can help.

— David Alev —

Once you and the client decide to work together, the focus in **Stage 2** shifts from proving you can do the job to getting the job done. In this section, you will establish your role as project manager. It's your job to attend to the client's goals by steering the client toward their vision of success while demystifying the process. By guiding the client through setting up systems, you transfer skills that will last a lifetime and cultivate a relationship that allows you to increase the chances things work long after you're gone.

Keep the Focus

I don't focus on what I'm up against.
I focus on my goals and I try to ignore the rest.

— Venus Williams —

When you show up for the appointment, you shift from talking to the client about the project to helping the client realize the stated goals. Continue to listen for opportunities to capture the client's wishes. The client will weave what's important to them into the conversation, and this will reinforce some of the earlier discussion you had on the phone. You want to continue to focus on why they want to work with you and why you are there.

Gentle persistence goes a long way toward managing project expectations throughout the relationship. Two of the most common problem areas are staying on track and punctually ending the session, which we will talk more about later.

Take Brenda as an example. She is a single woman who rarely gets the opportunity to talk to other adults. It's easy for her to get into the rhythm of organizing and have the process trigger a story she wants to share with me. I enjoy hearing the stories of her and her son's trip to the 1988 Summer Olympics in Seoul but will need to say, "If you still want the spare room ready for your son's visit next week, we need to refocus. Is there any chance you can continue your story while sorting through the pile?" At that point, she will make it clear I never have to apologize for bringing this to her attention because this observation is what she hired me to do for her: to help her stay focused on the project.

My job as the project manager/organizer is to keep my eyes focused on her goals. This is one of the hardest things for clients to do for themselves. Most appreciate the gentle nudge to stay focused on the predetermined goals. Face it: "Going down memory lane" is rarely a welcome line item on an invoice.

Projects are diverted in other ways. A project's rate for a room with an additional twelve boxes from the attic will change the scope of the project significantly. Project managers refer to this as "scope creep." Once a client goes off track, take the opportunity to see if they would like to change the goals for the session or project.

Depending on the size of the diversion, you may need to document the change of plans. This is another reason the **review** portion of your session is important. You and the client will see the additional work done and the changes to the plan that were necessary because of the scope creep. You guide; they decide.

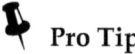 Pro Tip

You are a professional. Acknowledge scope creep and adjust the invoice accordingly.

Rookie Mistakes

- Working for free.
- Not ending the session on time.

The Focus Has Changed

*It is during our darkest moments
that we must focus to see the light.*

— Aristotle —

Let the client know when you notice the focus changing.

For example, a client calls you to talk about something weighing heavily on him, but when you get there, he wants to do something different. Let him know; say, "I came in to help with the office, and now we're doing the kitchen."

This gives him the opportunity to say "Let's switch to the new goal." Just letting the client know the focus has changed is a great way to manage expectations.

If you don't make it clear you noticed, your client may be disappointed with the results at the end of the session. If they called you in to do a home office and you get stuck in the primary bedroom closet for three hours, the office will not get done. There may be some frustration and hopelessness here. Take the opportunity to say "That's a great project, but you called for help in the office. I want to help you finish that space before we take on another project."

Many organizers tell stories of the focus changing, but they neglect to discuss the ramifications of the new direction with the client. Once the deliverables change, the scope of the job has changed. This will affect the time frame and budget, too. Document scope, budget, and time-altering changes on the invoice. In business, it's often called a *change order* and is a formal way to show the project scope has changed and ensures the client is aware of it.

Managing Client Expectations

Let the client know they can count on you to keep the project scope in mind at all times and you will help them maintain focus. Be conscientious about doing that. A quick and easy way to guarantee the session will be a success is to establish goals at the beginning of the session (the **talk**). While you are working, keep the goals in mind. If you need to put your goals in writing and refer to them, do so. I have clients for whom I write the goals on the invoice and put checkboxes next to them. We check them off as we complete them.

For example, working with a grieving client is an opportunity to acknowledge memories and let the client dictate how to proceed. If a client is determined to tell stories that derail the process, give them the choice to get back on track or to take a new path. In the end, everyone is happy.

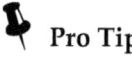 Pro Tip

Initiate a written *change order* when the project scope has changed. This can be noted on the invoice before you continue.

Power Questions

- *I came in to help with the garage, and now we're doing the kitchen. Do you want to stay with your original goal or do you want to change the focus?*
- *What can I do to help you stay on track?*

Mutual Respect and Value Judgments

For things to reveal themselves to us, we need to be ready to abandon our views about them.

— Thich Nhat Hanh —

Besides being responsible for how things are, you are also responsible for how your words are received and how your actions may appear. Always be respectful of your client's situation.

Rein in value judgments. Even a positive value judgment is a value judgment. When I enter a home for the first time, I never say "Wow, what a beautiful living room," even if I love it. The client is listening and processing every comment an organizer makes. A client will notice if I've made comments about the first four rooms and then say nothing when we get to the space where we will work.

Of course, stay away from comments that can be perceived as negative value judgments. For example, "Wow! Another craft magazine" can denote a negative connotation when it's not the intention. You're just surprised the craft industry had so many different magazines, but your client takes it as a personal judgment because they have countless unread magazines stacked around the house and aren't working on their craft projects.

Stay neutral at all times. Don't underestimate the power of your opinion with your clients.

When working with a client, say encouraging things. These statements support the client's progress and focus, but be aware of your words that judge choices and belongings. "You are working really hard" holds less judgment than "you are getting rid of a lot of stuff." Focus on the effort and not the stuff.

On another note, you want to avoid going to a new space and looking around as if you are scoping the place out for a heist. I experienced the awkward feeling when the guy who was hired to clean the carpet spent a lot of time commenting on my electronic equipment rather than focusing on the job he was hired to do. Why put our clients in this awkward position? If you are there to work on a filing system, you need not comment on their 65-inch TV.

You are also responsible for how things appear. Be aware of how your actions may appear to your client. For example, I was working in a client's bedroom and we were sorting through all of her jewelry when she left the room for a few minutes. My throat was getting dry and I wanted to get a mint from my purse, but I waited until she returned. I did not want the client to return to the room and see me zipping up my purse.

Of course, I knew I would not take anything. Out of respect for the client relationship, my industry, and my reputation, I wouldn't do anything that even appeared to jeopardize the client's trust.

Another case is when a client went to his storage unit while my team continued to work at the house. We planned to drop off the donations, and one of the team members suggested that it was a good time to load the car. Since the client was still out, I suggested we hold off and pointed out the value of waiting for the client to return. I explained that allowing the client to see precisely what's being removed so they won't wonder what they missed being taken from their home fosters peace of mind and trust.

In many long-term client relationships, this and many other tasks can be performed with a level of trust that's already been earned, which make scenarios like this no big deal.

Pro Tip

Point out client strengths by identifying the areas that are working and acknowledging what they have accomplished.

Business Strategy

- ❑ What are your go-to "pats on the back?"

Boundaries

*Self-image sets the boundaries
of individual accomplishment.*

— Maxwell Maltz —

Setting and maintaining professional boundaries is essential. It is your job to make these boundaries clear to the client. During the initial consultation, you should have made it clear what services you provide. During your sessions, you may need to remind the client that you are not a therapist or a housekeeper.

It's not uncommon for something personal to come up during a session and for a client to start to talk about it. You can say "This conversation is an excellent topic to talk over with your therapist." You can be sensitive to the client's feeling by pointing out that a better use of your time together is hands-on work. Focus on tasks the therapist does not perform.

If underlying issues are surfacing, there's nothing wrong with the client taking a moment to jot them down for later discussion in talk therapy. Maybe the client is experiencing grief around letting go. Additional training from any of the organizations that train professional organizers can help you master these situations with confidence. Some organizers even get training as grief counselors.

Keep in mind you may have to stop what you're working on and come back to it when the client feels more comfortable processing the task at hand.

Although I'm not a housekeeper, I will be the first to recommend grabbing a cloth to wipe down the shelves on the bookcase we just cleared. Before we return the books to the shelf, vacuuming behind the

Managing Client Expectations

bookcase makes sense. Understand, this is very different from vacuuming or dusting the entire room.

Before you ever work with the client, be clear about your job description. That alone can prevent any awkward situations before they ever arise. Don't ignore a situation expecting it to be a one-time occurrence. Differentiate what your job is and is not. Say something as simple as "Why don't I come in the day before the cleaner comes so they can clear out all the dust we kick up?" One, they know you will not perform the housekeeper job, and two, they now have a more realistic glimpse of how things will look when you leave.

When you notice clients making comments such as "We'll get this cleaned up," reframe it as "We will organize this, rather than clean it." Ensure clients don't use the term cleaning interchangeably with organizing. Keep the focus on implementing organizational systems and transferring skills, not making the space neater. You introduce systems that will make it easier to keep the room neat and clean in the long run.

Stage 2: The Middle

📌 Pro Tip

Respect boundaries, yours and theirs.

🚩 Rookie Mistake

Ignoring a situation and expecting it to be a one-time occurrence.

⚡ Power Questions

- *Would it be more helpful for you to talk this over with a therapist so we can continue with the hands-on work?*
- *Would you like to continue our work together after you sort out some of these issues?*
- *Why don't I come in the day before the cleaner comes so they can clear out all the dust we kick up?*

🛠 Business Strategy

- ❏ During the initial consultation, make your boundaries clear to the client.

Making Suggestions

Advice is like snow — the softer it falls, the longer it dwells upon, and the deeper it sinks into the mind.

— Samuel Taylor Coleridge —

As the professional consultant, you want to speak with confidence. Too often, this takes the form of "You should do this." It's so easy for us to "should" people because we consider ourselves experts. Taking a statement like "You should…" and turning it into "Have you considered…?" can change the dynamic. "Have you considered…?" is so much more inviting than "You should…." It opens the door to options just in case the client doesn't care for the idea. You could then follow up by saying "Well, it's just something I wanted you to consider. I have several other options that could be good fits for this particular situation."

Be gentle and matter-of-fact as you re-state expectations. You need to be heard, but your goal is to tuck in a little reality, not take away hope. As the relationship builds, continue to test assumptions and perform reality checks by restating what you heard and by asking "Did I get that right?" or "Does that make sense to you?" Use the same open-ended questioning you used in the phone consultation. You presented yourself as the expert on the phone, so you need to be the expert in person.

Look for the priorities that will make a client feel happy and accomplished after a session. Ask, "Is there anything you really want to get done today? Something you'll be happy we accomplished before I leave?"

Managing Client Expectations

📌 Pro Tip

Encourage problem-solving and brainstorming (sitting down with paper and pencil and mind-mapping a challenge).

⚡ Power Questions

- *Is there anything you really want to get done today?*
- *Did I get that right?*
- *Does that make sense to you?*
- *Have you considered...?*

Timekeeping

Lost time is never found again.

— Benjamin Franklin —

Help clients stay on task and on time. You'll learn that not only is it your responsibility to check the time often, it's also your job to talk about it out loud. Tell the client you're the timekeeper for the project. You are in charge of the time, so you will do periodic check-ins to pace the project using a smartphone timer. During these check-ins, tell your client:

"We're doing a good job. We're on task."

"Wow, it only took ten minutes to empty that box."

"Let's spend thirty minutes on this, then check back in."

These are excellent opportunities to model managing blocks of time.

Many professional organizers have difficulty figuring out the timing of sessions early in their practice. It's easy to lose track of time when you get engrossed in a project. At the beginning of my career, I wasn't always aware if I had been with a client for two hours or four hours. I wanted to check my watch without the client noticing. At the time, I thought letting the client see me check my watch implied I was bored and disinterested in the project at hand.

The expectation is that you're in charge of the time. If you need to look, by all means, look. Bring a reliable timepiece and show them how to manage their time. The client's clock may not work or have the correct time (which can be a project for a later session). No more trying to sneak a peek to avoid hurting a client's feeling about the length of time it's taking them to decide on something.

Managing Client Expectations

📌 **Pro Tip**

Timers are excellent tools to use while organizing. I use the Time Timer® brand timer. They offer an app and a physical timer.

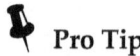 **Power Questions**

Use power statements like:

- *We're doing a good job. We're on task.*
- *Wow, it only took ten minutes to empty that box.*
- *Let's spend thirty minutes on this, then check back in.*

Remembering

We don't always need to recreate the wheel.
We just need to get things rolling.

— Anonymous —

Use your memory to help clients sift through choices. I'm constantly making mental notes about hobbies, preferences, strengths, challenges, and more while working with clients. If you prefer, you can make notes in their file after the session for future reference.

For instance, a client might say "I love knitting and want to knit more often." Later on, when she's clearing the closet in the guest room, you can say "This newfound space may be great for your yarn." She didn't realize you even heard her weeks earlier say she loves knitting, but returning to that shows her you were listening. When they say their kids' names, you want to weave that into the conversation later on, such as, "Maybe we can put those in John's room." Your client will be amazed you're actively listening and remembering a conversation from months ago.

One tenet of being a trusted advisor is remembering, without referring to your notes, everything they ever said. Try to remember their comments, no matter how small, so you can weave something encouraging into the conversation when the client needs it most.

Use the knowledge you've gathered from working and talking with your client to help them be successful. You want to remind them of their goals, motivations, and priorities (the what, why, and how of it).

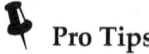 Pro Tips

Refer back to the client's values and goals at every session.

Right after you leave a client, while it's fresh in your mind, document any situation you feel you could have handled differently. Then learn from it.

✖ Business Strategy

- ❏ As soon as you get the chance, make a note of any procedural challenges that need to be addressed.

Listen to Input

You can't fake listening. It shows.

— Raquel Welch —

While you are rooting for the client to succeed, keep in mind, the client wants you to be successful, too. Why? Because you're on their team and they're rooting for you, too. They picked you. They're going to help you out as much as possible. You will get clues to be successful, so listen up; clients are continually giving you valuable information you can use.

New clients may not always feel comfortable telling you what they thought about the session if they are not satisfied. Framing questions that won't put them on the spot is helpful. Don't ask, "Did you like that?" or "Wasn't that great?" If they weren't satisfied with the experience, they may not always come out and say so. Look for clues and ask open-ended questions that will help you get the information you need to change the course of the appointment or structure future appointments. Ask something along the lines of, "This is your first experience with an organizer. How was the session different than what you anticipated?" or "What are your takeaways from today?"

Watch their body language and the way a client is acting to gauge their thoughts. You can tell by the way a client gets their checkbook whether or not they are excited. Or the client may say "Wow, we worked so hard, I'm so tired." I personally love hearing clients got a good workout during the session.

By the way, observe your own body language to be sensitive to how you appear. Are your arms folded like their parent or are you standing over them like a demanding boss?

📌 Pro Tips

Be aware of how you ask "why" questions, the tone of your voice and your body language.

Be observant of a client's body language and keep an open ear for comments that suggest their state of mind.

⚡ Power Questions

- *This is your first experience with an organizer; what worked for you today?*
- *What would you like to do differently next time?*
- *What did we spend time doing that was different than what you initially wanted to do?*

Stage 2: The Middle

Finish on a High Note

A good plan today is better than a perfect plan tomorrow. Don't wait for an inspired ending to come to mind. Work your way to the ending and see what comes up.

— Andy Weir —

Finish on a high note by reinforcing accomplishments and celebrating results.

The last hour of the session is key to finishing on a high note. During the entire session, keep a mental image of the end. Design your sessions so the last hour includes the following steps:

- Wrap things up so the space is "usable" after you're gone.
- Perform any rituals that signify a job well done and celebrate results.
- Recap work done during the session.
- Reinforce any systems you put in place.

Get a client to say, "We always do this..." Creating rituals for the end of the appointment will endear you to the client. The client knows you are on their team. There's something familiar about continuing with an end-of-session ritual. Try to create some with your clients.

One of my clients celebrates by counting the trash bags she fills during the session. She wants to line them up like soldiers so she can walk by, look at them, and feel the accomplishment of a job well done. I always put on her invoice how many we filled. She counts them again, and then we take them to the dumpster. We throw them over and we do a "high five."

Keep the momentum going and let clients know they can use rituals to perform tasks between visits. Consider having the client tie a task they don't enjoy to a task they do enjoy. Sorting mail while watching a comedy on TV is an example of batching a more difficult task with an easy one. To this day, I motivate myself to organize my purse while I enjoy catching up with my mother over the phone.

📌 **Pro Tips**

Reminder: this is a part of the **review** portion of **walk, talk, do, review**

Help clients create their own rituals.

Reassure the client that if there's time left over after the review, you will do a mini project. There's always a mini project to be done.

🚩 **Rookie Mistakes**

- Not managing the time properly and leaving the workspace worse than when you started.

- Not realizing that putting things back and doing a **review** are part of the organizing session.

- Working until the last minute and not having time to wrap things up and set it up for the next time.

- Failing to see the importance of the last hour of recapping and **review**.

⚒ **Business Strategy**

- ❏ What are some rituals most of your clients could establish before, during, and after the session?

Invoicing

You don't get paid for the hour.
You get paid for the value you bring to the hour.

— Jim Rohn —

Write down everything you did on the invoice at the end of the session. Ask the client to help you remember what you did together so they can recite accomplishments out loud. By helping you recall the details of the session, the client gets another opportunity to review progress. The client is happy to write that check after going down the laundry list of accomplishments. Hearing my client say "We did this. Oh, you helped me with that. And we did that, and we did that…" is a nice lead-in to getting paid.

Use the invoicing time as an opportunity to give tips and point out things that clients can do to keep up the momentum, so they are less likely to backslide.

Here's a lead-in to this maintenance talk:

> "These are the things we worked on…. This is how you can maintain it…. Maintaining the new system will be a realistic goal until the next visit."

Do your invoice during the **review** time. If you work in three-hour segments with a client, you're actually doing the bill paying, scheduling, and review during the session. Not afterward. Don't work for three hours and then spend another twenty minutes with the client.

Refer back to the chapter, Session Scenario: **Walk, Talk, Do,** and **Review** on page 31. You have already told them invoicing would be part of the review portion of the session so nothing here should be a surprise.

Managing Client Expectations

Once the invoice has been presented and paid, you still have client expectations to deal with. Given the scenario below, think about what you could have done differently in the various stages.

Scenario: You just finished your first session with a new client and handed him the invoice. You are about to grab some lunch before your next appointment, but your new client stops you at the door looking distressed. He's upset he spent so much of the session telling you about a recent fight with his ex-wife. He's anxious the spare bedroom wasn't finished today, revealing he needs it this weekend for his visiting kids, and he asks for some tips on completing the room himself. Before you can respond, he adds this: "By the way, I wanted wicker baskets for the shelves, not plastic bins. Can you bring them before the end of today?"

🛠 Business Strategies

From the scenario above:

- ❏ What could you have done in your client conversations to avoid this situation?
- ❏ What could you have done during the session to prevent this last-minute regret?
- ❏ What could you have done during the invoicing process to be aware of his dissatisfaction?
- ❏ Now that this happened, what would you do to fix this?

Stage 3

The End of the Appointment and the Beginning of a Lasting Relationship

As human beings, our greatness lies not so much in being able to remake the world... as in being able to remake ourselves.

— Mahatma Gandhi —

Finally, in **Stage 3**, we'll examine the end of the appointment and the beginning of a solid client relationship. More importantly, Stage 3 explores how you can get the job done without feeling as if you depleted your energy. A solid client relationship opens the door to an abundance of choices for next steps, whether it's continuing with other organizing projects, referrals, maintenance work, or just a long-lasting admiration for the work accomplished. You will never hesitate to check in with the client, and your professionalism will help define you as a *go-to* organizer for years to come.

The Cost of Doing Business

Opportunity is missed by most people because it is dressed in overalls, and looks like work.

— Thomas Edison —

You can line item everything, but it may not be in your best interest to charge the client an additional fee for every little thing. Some things are just the cost of doing business. Decide what things you do for a client that will be included in the cost of doing business, and what you will invoice above and beyond your hourly rate or project rate.

For example, when I'm setting up filing systems or sorting through papers with clients, I'll re-use inexpensive, single-ply file folders to pre-sort paper. I buy them in bulk from a warehouse store, and I don't charge the client for the folders. Once we have final label names and categories established, we switch to a more substantial product for the permanent file. The temporary file folders are just reusable sorting tools.

Similarly, if I make two or three labels on the job with my label maker, even at the high cost of label tape, I would not expect the client to pay a surcharge for each label. On the other hand, if I create a comprehensive filing system with printed labels, in addition to the time expense, I would expect the client to pay for the folders and rolls of label tape.

Managing Client Expectations

 Pro Tip

Even if there are no additional charges associated with the supplies or work you do on a project, make a notation on the invoice. Demonstrate the full worth of your work, and let the client realize the value of working with you and your company.

Business Strategies

- What services and supplies do you consider part of doing business?
- Have you calculated the cost of those things into your hourly or project rate?
- Do you have additional fees you pass on to your clients above and beyond your hourly or project rate?
- When you offer something for free that otherwise could be an expense, do you list it on your invoice as a line item?
- What notation do you use next to the complimentary items? "No charge"? "N/C"?
- How do you note discounts for supplies or services on your invoice?

Stage 3: The End & The Beginning

The Car Hostage

Comfortable shoes and the freedom to leave are the two most important things in life.

— Shel Silverstein —

Avoid being a "car hostage." I got this term from a colleague in the San Francisco Bay Area. In New England, the weather lends itself more toward the "foyer hostage."

Sometimes clients will see us all the way to the car or the door and then want to talk for twenty minutes. Have the appointment end in a professional manner.

Create your end-of-session routine to allow you to leave on time. Don't set the expectation that you talk for thirty minutes after your appointments. This ritual can complicate the relationship and send the wrong message. You don't want to start something you can't continue after every appointment. Don't send the message that there is a complimentary question-and-answer session after every appointment. The day you can't sit and talk, the client will wonder if something is wrong.

When the client initially called you, they did not come to you looking for friendship; they came to you because of your expertise in productivity. You are a professional businessperson, and once you've done your job and you've been paid, in most cases, it's time to go.

Establish clear boundaries between work and friendship. Remember, you can be friendly with your client without being their friend. (No need to send me your unique situation. I know there are circumstances when a client becomes a friend or the client was a friend before they hired you. I get it.)

Managing Client Expectations

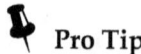 **Pro Tip**

It's okay to tell the client you have another appointment. Even if your next stop is called "lunch." You deserve to have a break before your next engagement.

Stage 3: The End & The Beginning

Dressing the Part

A man should look as if he had bought his clothes with intelligence, put them on with care, and then forgotten all about them.

— Hardy Amies —

When a client opens the door and sees you for the first time, do your appearance and demeanor reflect the client's expectations of you and your company?

The aim here is to meet the expectations of the job, model a put-together look, and dress appropriately for the task at hand. When it's time to roll up your sleeves, clients need to know you don't mind digging in to get the job done. If the client had any concerns about investing in your services, would they feel reassured if the first impression you made was in jeans, a tee-shirt, and flip-flops?

In my experience, in addition to a website and phone conversation, judgments of our professionalism are established based on appearance. Imagine walking into a medical establishment for a procedure and having the doctor you have never met before put you at ease by showing up bedside with dirty hands and in jeans and a tank top. In response to your surprise, he complains it's a messy job, and he doesn't want to dirty up his "good" pants. How would that make you feel?

Moving from New England to the West Coast helped soften my views over the years. If a client comments on your outfit, you may want to rethink some of your choices. I once had a client who thought I was dressed too nicely to work in her garage. I took a moment to assure her there was no need to worry. In my practice, my goal is to present myself as neutrally as possible.

For residential work, I wear an outfit that easily goes into the washing machine and can handle some wear and tear. I look for outfits that are professional and represent my brand, but that can take a beating. I choose my outfits so I can work anywhere.

The way I dress for a desk-side office job is different from how I would dress to organize a garage. A "desk-side job" is an industry term for working with an executive desk-side. I am in their office and may be talking to the client while they sit at the computer. I may be working with files, but it isn't dirty work.

Our company policy is not to wear jeans, or to have exposed toes, armpits, or belly buttons. For some special-needs clients, something as simple as the movement from a pair of dangle earrings, shoes that squeak, or fabric that creates sounds with every moment can be a distraction.

Throughout this book, I give you real-life experiences from my practice and challenge you to come up with solutions that work for you. You don't have to wear what I wear. What's important is that you give serious thought to what you wear because you are making an impression the moment you walk through the door.

Stage 3: The End & The Beginning

📌 Pro Tips

- Wear situationally appropriate clothing.

- Invest in yourself. Meet with an image consultant if you need to spruce up your business image.

- Be aware of the needs and sensibilities of your client.

🏳 Rookie Mistakes

- Neglecting safety standards such as failing to wear gloves or a mask because you don't want to hurt the client's feelings.

- Not encouraging your client to take the same precautions.

🛠 Business Strategies

When a client opens the door and sees you for the first time, do your appearance and demeanor reflect the client's expectations of you and your company?

What is your message:

- ☐ Does your work attire match your branding?
- ☐ Does your work attire match the job you are there to do?
- ☐ Does your work attire protect your body?
- ☐ Does your work attire represent a well-organized closet?

Organizers' Expectations

Follow the three Rs: Respect for self, respect for others, responsibility for all your actions.

— Dalai Lama —

Keep the focus on the job at hand. Seasoned organizers know it pays to take time to reflect on their own expectations going into any project even if it's not the first time working with the client.

Our misplaced expectations cause frustration with what we perceive as a client's lack of progress. Those feelings have more to do with us than with the client. This process also reminds us we don't have all the answers for a particular client's project. Managing our own expectations—and challenging underlying assumptions—empowers us to do the same for our clients.

In the words of George Bernard Shaw, "…conduct is influenced not by our experience, but by our expectations." Whether those expectations are "yours," "mine," or "ours," success in managing expectations requires clear two-way communication. This communication begins with the understanding that our clients need and want to be heard. It continues with patient education and guidance, and is cemented by the examples we set.

📌 Pro Tip

Recognize professional organizers are human. Keep realistic expectations for yourself, and know sometimes you need to *let go to grow*.

Follow-Up

If you don't know where you're going,
any road will take you there.

— Lewis Carroll —

There are many ways to follow up between visits or after a project is complete. You could offer maintenance sessions, coaching calls, or email support to the client between visits.

You can also start subsequent appointments with follow-up questions, such as:

- How did you manage the systems we implemented between visits?
- Were you able to work on the homework assignments you wanted to complete?
- What worked best for you?
- What did not work for you?

Homework

When a client requests you assign homework between visits, it's important to keep in mind that oftentimes you were initially called because the client was having difficulties completing the project on their own. The client's overwhelm and need for guidance may not disappear after one visit.

Figure out why you were brought in and assign homework accordingly. If a client brought you in for strategic direction, then taking on tasks between appointments may come easy. On the other hand, if organizing is a lifelong struggle, taking on complicated tasks between visits in the beginning may not be as easily mastered.

Whatever the reason for the client's initial call, be mindful of this when offering suggestions for homework a client can work on between visits. It is always my intention to design systems that will continue to serve the client long after I'm gone. To transfer skills, tailor your systems to match the client's needs.

If you were working on a client's closet, *homework* examples would be:

- Gather up all the black pants and get them ready to be sorted the next time.
- Empty drawers before the next appointment.
- Research charities important to them for donations.
- Brainstorm how they want to use the space so there's more clarity during the work session.
- Call their children to find out what they may want.

Extra credit homework: Have the client maintain the accomplishments of your last visit. Maintaining systems takes effort. Reinforce the notion that getting organized is not a one-time function, but rather a lifestyle change. Living an organized life is an ongoing process requiring you to maintain the implemented systems. Celebrate keeping *things in place*.

I call homework that's not maintaining a system you put in place "money savers" which are things client can do on their own to save money and reduce the expenses while working with you.

Stage 3: The End & The Beginning

📌 Pro Tip

Set your client up for success. Be aware of your client's strengths and weaknesses and suggest appropriate between-visit assignments.

 Power Questions

- *How did you manage the systems we implemented?*
- *How did your homework go?*
- *What worked best for you?*
- *What did not work for you?*

🛠 Business Strategy

❏ Make a list of "money savers" you can offer to a client before, during, and after the appointment.

Self-Care

As human beings, our greatness lies not so much in being able to remake the world... as in being able to remake ourselves.

— Mahatma Gandhi —

How do you treat yourself? Are you living up to the standards you expect from your clients? Are you living what you preach day in and day out? Simply put, are you taking your own advice?

Taking care of yourself will make you a better organizer, coach, consultant, business owner, employee, parent, friend, partner, committee member, and of course a better you. Your clients expect it! You want to attract clients to your business who expect you to have a life filled with adequate relaxation. Your clients expect you make time to care for your health, visit your health care providers, eat healthy meals to support your energy level, and hydrate your body for clarity in thinking.

When is the last time you took a vacation? A real vacation—where you turned off your phone and left your laptop at home? A vacation where you didn't spend time working indoors while your family was at the pool? Yes, boundaries can be an issue for organizers too, as I mentioned in Stage 1, Time Frame. Does your business have hours of operation, or are you sitting at your desk at 10 p.m. sending emails while the rest of the family is curled up on the couch watching a movie? I often tell my clients one of the benefits of being organized is time for family and friends. I have to remind myself often that this applies to me, too.

Self-care includes doing what you enjoy. An organizer in my NAPO* chapter shared with me that she has no desire to deal with the day-to-

---

* NAPO: National Association of Productivity and Organizing Professionals™

day business aspects of the company she owns. She much prefers "hands-on organizing" rather than "bringing new clients to the business." At the annual NAPO conference, she sent one of her employees to the breakout sessions on "how to run an organizing business" while she concentrated on the "how to be a better organizer" breakouts. This is an excellent example of an ideal situation that supports her lifestyle and career choices. Besides creating a fantastic working environment, she has created an environment with employees who support each other's strengths and interests.

Lastly, and most importantly, pay yourself. Your ideal clients expect you to pay yourself. This is the ultimate in self-care. Set up a payment system, whatever works for you, but make sure you get paid. Set aside money for retirement. If you are not doing it, do it! You can thank me in thirty years when you're sitting on a nice little nest egg from the compound interest. You would not expect your clients to work for free or to be unprepared for the future; nor should you accept that for yourself.

🔧 Business Strategies

- How are you practicing self-care?
- When is the last time you took a vacation?
- How often are you delegating tasks you don't enjoy doing?
- How do you dig yourself out of a rut?
- What advice do you give clients that you need to take yourself?

Stage 3: The End & The Beginning

Now What?

*The journey of a thousand miles
begins with one step.*

— Lao Tzu —

Now that you've invested your time in reading this book, identify what needs to change in your practice. Some things will need to be modified immediately, and others will transform as you grow your business. Combine the knowledge you have gained from reading *Managing Client Expectations: A Guide for Organizing Professionals* with your life experience, relationship skills, and investigative skills to further develop your client relationships.

⚒ Business Strategies

- ❏ What do you want to keep doing in your practice?
- ❏ What do you want to stop doing in your practice?
- ❏ What do you want to start doing in your practice?
- ❏ Where do you need to establish boundaries in your practice?
- ❏ What tasks are inappropriate for clients to expect you to do?
- ❏ What makes you a good professional organizer?
- ❏ What are your personal goals for increasing client satisfaction through managing expectations?
- ❏ What are some clues you can look for to judge if the session was a success?
- ❏ What are some techniques you can use to ensure clients are satisfied with the results?
- ❏ What are some difficult topics for you to discuss with potential clients?

Traits Trusted Advisors Have in Common[†]

You want to become a trusted advisor for your client. As you read this list, consider yourself the trusted advisor and read from a client's point of view.

Trusted Advisors:

Seem to understand us, effortlessly, and like us

Are consistent (we can depend on them)

Always help us see things from fresh perspectives

Don't try to force things on us

Help us think things through (it's our decision)

Don't substitute their judgment for ours

Don't panic or get overemotional (they stay calm)

Help us think and separate our logic from our emotion

Criticize and correct us gently, lovingly

Don't pull their punches (we can rely on them to tell us the truth)

Are in it for the long haul (the relationship is more important than the current issue)

Give us reasoning (to help us think), not just their conclusions

---

[†] This list is excerpted from The Trusted Advisor. It is used with permission of the author, David Maister.

Give us options, increase our understanding of those options, give us their recommendations, and let us choose

Challenge our assumptions (help us uncover the false assumptions we've been working under)

Make us feel comfortable and casual personally (but they take the issues seriously)

Act like a real person, not someone in a role

Are reliably on our side and always seem to have our interest at heart

Remember everything we ever said (without notes)

Are always honorable (they don't gossip about others, and we trust their values)

Help us put our issues in context, often through the use of metaphors, stories, and anecdotes (few problems are unique)

Have a sense of humor to diffuse (our) tension in tough situations

Are smart (sometimes in ways we are not)

Resources

Associations

Your association's code of ethics is a great resource to develop the policies and procedures for your business, especially for newcomers to the industry. These guidelines, mostly aspirational, are an excellent set of principles for managing expectations and setting boundaries for your practice. You will work with integrity and do the work you are qualified to do. Talk now, save time, and have happy clients later.

NAPO® — National Association of Productivity and Organizing Professionals™

APPO — Association of Personal Photo Organizers

ICD — Institute for Challenging Disorganization®

NASMM — National Association of Senior Move Managers®

IFPOA — International Federation of Professional Organizing Associations

Brazil: ANPOP — Associação Nacional de Profissionais de Organização e Produtividade

Canada: POC — Professional Organizers in Canada

Japan: JALO — Japan Association of Life Organizers

Netherlands: NBPO — Nederlandse Beroepsvereniging van Professional Organizers

Republic of Korea: KAPO — Korean Association of Professional Organizers

United Kingdom: APDO — Association of Professional Declutterers & Organisers

Books

Karten, Naomi. *Managing Expectations: Working with People Who Want More, Better, Faster, Sooner, NOW!*. New York: Dorset House, 1994.

Maister, David H., Charles H. Green, and Robert M. Galford. *The Trusted Advisor*. New York: The Free Press (Simon & Schuster, Inc.), 2000.

Additional Resources

Alev, David. "Manage Expectations or Expect to be Managed, Part 1 and Part 2," The Consulting Academy, accessed as online course in 2003 at http://consultingacademy.com

Quotes:
  www.brainyquote.com
  www.goodreads.com
  www.azquotes.com

Things In Place®, www.thingsinplace.com (redirects to standolyn.com)

About the Author

Don't lower your expectations to meet your performance. Raise your level of performance to meet your expectations. Expect the best of yourself, and then do what is necessary to make it a reality.

– Ralph Marston –

Standolyn Robertson (pronounced Stan-doh-lin, rhymes with Mandolin)–Certified Professional Organizer, speaker, featured expert for major print & TV outlets, and adorer of art, great food, and adventure.

Since founding Things In Place® in 2000, she has connected with thousands of clients and organizations through her coaching, consulting, workshops, and talks. She has also served as president of the National Association of Productivity & Organizing Professionals, and has been featured in the *New York Times*, the *Wall Street Journal*, *Woman's Day*, *Family Circle*, *Real Simple*, *USA Today*, the *Boston Globe*, the *LA Times*, and *Money Magazine*, as well as on CBS, NPR, the Emmy-nominated show "Hoarders" and more.

As an organizer and a coach, Standolyn operates under a single, simple philosophy: clear spaces, clear minds. With her comprehensive, personalized strategies, she combines wisdom with practical concepts and whip-smart tactics to help women and men around the world take back control of their lives, their values, and their happiness.

For more from Standolyn, stop by www.ThingsInPlace.com, www.Standolyn.com, or drop her a line at Standolyn@thingsinplace.com.

If you found this book useful, consider leaving a review on Amazon. It helps others find this book.

www.ingramcontent.com/pod-product-compliance
Lightning Source LLC
Chambersburg PA
CBHW051322220526
45468CB00004B/1456